JOKING

What's the definition of
    Stevie Wonder and F

* * *

What do you get when you cross a Mexican and
an Italian?
    A guy who makes you an offer you can't
understand!

* * *

What's a J A P's idea of perfect sex?
    Simultaneous headaches!

* * *

Why do Jewish men die before their wives do?
    Because they want to!

* * *

Misery is finding out that your son has gone into
law enforcement . . . as a meter maid!

* * *

Love is a many gendered thing!

Also in the Series

Joking Off 1

JOKING OFF
2

Johnny Lyons

Virgin

A Virgin Book
Published in 1989
by the Paperback Division of
W. H. Allen & Co. Plc
44 Hill Street, London W1X 8LB

First published in the USA by PaperJacks

Copyright © 1987 by Lion Entertainment, Inc.

Printed and bound in Great Britain by
Cox & Wyman Ltd, Reading

ISBN 0 86369 306 7

This book is dedicated to all people who love jokes! Particularly to my many friends, business associates and acquaintances who have been generous with their jokes with me over the years.

Those include:

C. Lyons (my wonderful mother), Suzanne and Bernie L., Harold, Foul Al, Alexander and Ted A., Michael B., Vincent B., Jonathan B., Lamar C., Helen D., Robin S., Mike, Steve, C.C.G., Costas K., Sandy L., Albert M., Pee Wee, Raul N., Richmond R., Lazaris Z., Susan, the Postman, the Cab drivers of the City of New York, the Bartenders of the World, Johnny Zero, to Bob for listening, and especially Tony the U.P.S. man, and a very special thanks to Vincent C.

TABLE OF CONTENTS

Sex, Drugs
And
Rock 'N' Roll

Two honeymooners go away to a hunting lodge in the backwoods. The husband develops the strange habit of getting up every morning at five o'clock and going out. Some of the lodge employees notice this and one of them says to the guy, "Why do you leave your wife every morning when you should be making love?" The husband says, "My wife has gonorrhea." "That's no problem. Why doesn't she give you a blow-job?" "She has pyorrhea." Exasperated, the employee says, "Then why don't you give it to her up the ass?" "She has diarrhea. And the reason I'm going fishing all the time is she has worms too."

* * *

What's the definition of gross?

When a varsity cheerleader does a split and eight class rings fall out!

Two statues were set free by two angels and were told that they could have an hour off and go out and do whatever they wanted to for sixty minutes. They left and immediately found some pigeons and shit all over them. They were back in twenty-five minutes, and the angels said, "Why did you come back so early?" and the statues said, "We finished what we had to do."

* * *

A guy walks into a bar, goes up to the bartender and orders a beer. He drinks half the beer and pours the other half on his hand. The bartender watches him. So the guy orders another beer, and again he drinks half of it and pours the other half on his hand. Then he does it again with a third beer. The bartender's watching him the whole time, and finally the bartender says, "Are you going to order another beer?" And the guy says, "Yeah." "And are you going to pour half of it on your hand?" And the guy says, "Yeah." "Well, what the hell are you doing?" the bartender asks him. "Well," the guy says, "I want to make sure my date is as drunk as I am."

* * *

A man and a woman have been married for thirty years, and all that time the wife has kept a locked chest at the foot of the bed, and the husband has never looked in it. Finally the husband says, "Honey, in all these thirty years that we've been married, I've never asked you what's in the chest. So tell me — what is it?" And the woman says, "Well, we've been married thirty years. Here's the key; look for yourself." So the husband opens the chest and sees three ears of corn and a whole lot of cash inside. So the husband says, "Honey, what are the three ears of corn for?" The wife says, "Well, every time I had an indiscretion I put an ear of corn in the chest." "Well, that's not so bad," says the husband. "Thirty years and three indiscretions. But what's all the money for?" And the wife says, "Well, every time I filled the chest with corn, I took it out and sold it!"

* * *

A priest, a minister and a rabbi get together and talk about the issue of when life begins. The priest begins by saying, "I think life begins at the precise moment the sperm fertilizes the egg." The minister says, "Well, I think life begins at the precise moment the baby's bottom is smacked and it draws its first breath." And then the rabbi says, "Well, I think life begins when the dog has died and the children have moved out of the house."

* * *

An elderly couple goes to the doctor's office because the man is having trouble with his prostate gland. He's in the doctor's office and the doctor says to him, "Do you and your wife have intercourse?" And the old man says, "Wait, I'll ask my wife." So he goes to the door and yells, "Honey, do we have intercourse?" And the wife yells back, "No! We have Blue Cross!"

* * *

A single girl picks up a guy and they go back to her place. All of a sudden the guy is coming on to her, and the girl says that she's very paranoid about herpes and AIDS and all the diseases that are running rampant in today's society, and would he mind using his big toe? And the guy says, "Well, I have my clothes off and everything, and I'm really turned on. Why not." So the guy uses his big toe. A couple of weeks later the guy notices that his toe is infected, so he goes to a doctor and says, "What is wrong with my toe?" And the doctor says, "I can't believe it. The strangest medical things have been happening to me lately. You won't believe this, but you have gonorrhea of the toe." And the guy says, "Oh, no! I can't believe it." And the doctor says, "Well, that's not too bad. A couple of weeks ago I had a woman in here with athlete's foot in her cunt!"

* * *

Three surgeons come out of their respective operating rooms, and one surgeon says to the other, "Well, I just operated on an accountant. It was really easy — all the organs in this accountant's body were numbered." The second surgeon says, "Well, *I* just operated on an engineer, and not only were all the organs numbered, but they were also color-coded!" The third surgeon says, "Well, I just operated on an attorney, and it was the easiest surgery I have ever done. This guy only had two organs in his entire body — and they were both assholes!"

* * *

A guy takes a girl out on a first date, and they have a great time. He takes her to dinner, then he takes her to a show, then he takes her out dancing.

At the end of the evening, she proceeds to shake his hand and then goes into her apartment. The guy goes berserk, breaks down her door, chases her all over the place, rips off her dress and has sex with her. Afterward, he's very pleased with himself. "I could tell you loved it," he says to her. "I knew it when I saw your toes curl up." "You asshole," says the girl. "You know why my toes curled up? You never took off my panty hose!"

* * *

A husband and wife are riding around town, and the wife says to her husband, "See that hotel? We own it." The husband says, "How do we own it?" And the wife says, "See that movie house over there? We own that too." The husband says, "I really don't understand." The wife says, "Keep driving and I'll show you some more properties that we own." The husband says, "What is this all about?" The wife says, "Remember every time you made love to me over the year you gave me $10.00. Well, I saved it all up and I invested in all these properties." The husband says, "Too bad I didn't do all my screwing at home — we'd own the whole town by now!"

* * *

The Pope decides to put on some civilian clothes and go out into the street incognito. While he's out walking, this woman comes up to him and says, "Want a blow-job?" The Pope says, "A blow-job? What's that?" And the woman says, "Ten dollars." As the Pope proceeds through the streets, he's barraged by many women saying, "Blow-job," "Blow-job," all day long. He finally returns to the papal palace and asks one of the nuns, "Tell me, Sister, what's a 'blow-job'?" "Ten dollars," says the nun.

* * *

A rather bookish young man goes into a whorehouse to seek entertainment. He goes up to the madam and says, "Madam, I'd like a woman for the evening." The madam says, "Sir, I'm afraid all the girls are taken tonight, but if you'd care to, I'm available." So the guy and the madam go into a bedroom and get undressed. As he takes off his clothes, she looks him over and she notices that, flaccid, he's only two inches long. But then the guy says, "Rise, Caesar!" And his cock rises to a full twelve inches. So they have a great time, and after about five hours the madam is very impressed. "Sir," she says, "this has been one of the most pleasurable evenings of my life. I was wondering if you'd mind if I called the girls in so they could have a look at you. You're really something special, you know." But the guy says, "No, madam, no. I have come to bury Caesar, not to praise him."

* * *

Cinderella is scrubbing the floors one night, and sobbing because she can't go to the ball. Lo and behold, the good fairy appears and asks her what is the matter. "I have nothing to wear to the ball tonight!" says Cinderella. "Well, I can fix that," says the good fairy, and with a wave of her wand she creates a beautiful ball dress. "Now, there's just one thing," says the good fairy. "You have to be home by midnight. If you're late, a terrible thing will happen — your pussy will turn into a pumpkin!"

"Oh, thank you, fairy godmother!" says Cinderella, and she gets dressed and goes to the ball. Once there, she meets a gorgeous prince and spends the whole evening dancing. Of course, she forgets about the time — until, just before midnight, she glances at the clock and jumps up in horror. "Wait!" cries the prince. "I don't even know your name!" "It's Cinderella!" yells Cinderella. "What's yours?" "Peter, Peter, Pumpkin-Eater," says the guy, and Cinderella stops in her tracks. "What am I running for?" says Cinderella, and they live happily ever after.

* * *

A state trooper notices a car weaving in the road, and when he pulls it over a beautiful woman gets out. She is clearly under the influence, but just to make sure he gives her the breathalyzer test. Sure enough, she's over the limit, so the trooper says, "Madam, you've had a couple of stiff ones." "Oh," says the lady, "it shows that too?"

* * *

Once there was a woman who loved country singers. She loved them so much she decided to have her two favorites tattooed on her body. So she went to the tattoo parlor and had the artist tattoo a portrait of Wayne Newton on one thigh and Elvis Presley on the other, way up on the insides of her legs. So the woman went home and said to her husband, "Look what I had done at the tattoo parlor!" And the guy said, "Yeah, that's a really good picture of Wayne Newton. And I have never seen a better likeness of Johnny Cash." "You dummy," said the lady, "that isn't Johnny Cash. That's Elvis Presley." "That's Johnny Cash." "It's Elvis Presley!" They went around and around on this for a while, and finally decided to go back to the tattoo parlor and ask the artist himself. When they got there, however, the artist was gone and there was just an old man minding the store. So they asked the old man to look at the woman's thighs and tell them exactly what he saw. "Well," said the old man, "that sure is Wayne Newton on the left there. And that sure is Johnny Cash on the right. And as for the one in the middle — that sure as hell looks like Willie Nelson to me!"

* * *

A man has an undying love for his wife, and to express it he decides to get a tattoo. So he goes to the tattoo parlor and looks over the various designs, but he can't find anything that suits him. Finally the manager suggests, "Why not have 'I Love You' tattooed on your penis?" "Hey, that's a great idea," says the guy, and has it done. That night in bed, he throws back the covers and shows his wife what he's done for her. "How about that?" says the guy. "What do you think of it? Pretty great, huh?"

"There you go again!" says the wife. "Always trying to put words in my mouth!"

* * *

How do you know if you've had oral sex the night before?

If, when you wake up in the morning, your face looks like a glazed doughnut!

What has 312 teeth and guards a giant?
  My zipper!

* * *

What has eighteen legs and two tits?
  The Supreme Court!

* * *

There are four nuns, and they're up in heaven, at the pearly gates. They're very nervous about getting into heaven, and Saint Peter says, "Well, you don't have to be worried; you're all women of the cloth, and you just have to tell me if you've ever committed any sins." So the first nun comes up and she says, "Well, Saint Peter, I have to tell you that once, with my right forefinger, I touched a man's penis." Saint Peter says, "This is not a problem; you shouldn't be embarrassed about that. I want you to just bathe your finger in holy water." There's a fountain of holy water nearby, so the nun goes and sticks her finger in the holy water, and Saint Peter says, "Fine, now you're admitted to heaven." Then the second nun comes up to him and says, "Saint Peter, I must confess that once I held a man's penis in my left hand." And Saint Peter says, "No problem. Just go over and immerse your hand in the holy water." So she does, and the saint says, "Fine, now you can go to heaven. Who's next?" The fourth nun steps out in front of the third nun and says, "Saint Peter, I don't mean to be pushy, but I just thought, if I'm going to have to wash my mouth out in that water I'd rather do it before she sits in it!"

An old man is sitting on a park bench, and he's crying his eyes out. He's maybe eighty years old, and finally a policeman comes over and asks him what's the problem. "I just got married," sobs the old man, "to a beautiful young woman. Every morning she gets up and cooks my breakfast, and then we make love. And then at lunchtime she makes me a wonderful lunch, and then we make love. And then at night she cooks me a beautiful dinner, and then we make love for hours!" And the old man sobs as if his heart will break. "What the hell is the matter with you?" asks the policeman. "You have a beautiful young wife who's a terrific cook and all the sex anyone could want. What are you crying about?" And the old man sobs, "I can't remember where I live!"

* * *

A woman gets a new job working in a sperm bank, and her friends ask her what she does. She says, "Well, I just sit in the reception area and greet all the men who come in — it's mainly men. Women never come in there — and I act cordial. And I point out to the men where they should go, and when they come out, I say, 'Thank you for coming'!"

* * *

A Catholic golfer goes to confession, and he's sitting with the priest in the confessional. He says, "And also, Father, I'd like to be forgiven for swearing. I swore the other day out on the golf course." The priest says, "Well, that's understandable, my son. Golf is a frustrating game, and it's filled with all kinds of disappointments. Would you care to tell me what happened?" And the guy says, "Well, Father, it was like this. My friend and I were all tied up at the eighteenth hole, and I bet him $100 that I could beat him on the last hole. I teed up and hit the ball, and my tee shot went right in the woods." "Oh," said the priest, "and that's when you swore. Well, that's understandable, my son, with all that money riding on the game." But the guy says, "No! The ball went in the woods, but it hit a tree and bounced back onto the fairway. But then it landed in the sand trap next to the green." "Oh, I understand, my son," says the priest. "That's when you swore, of course — when it went in the sand trap." "No, no," says the guy, "that's not when I swore. You see, after it landed in the trap, it hit a rake and bounced up onto the green and landed only twelve inches away from the hole!" So the priest thinks about it for a minute, and then says, "Don't tell me you missed the fucking putt!"

* * *

Did you hear about the woman who told her boyfriend, "Give me nine inches and make it hurt!"

He fucked her twice and slapped her in the face.

* * *

Why did God invent booze?

So ugly girls could get laid too.

* * *

What do control-top panty hose and Brooklyn have in common?

Flatbush!

A guy is driving through the country and his car breaks down. He sees a farmhouse in the distance, so he goes over and knocks on the door. A little kid comes to the door, and the guy says, "My car just broke down and I'd like to use your telephone. Is your mom home?" And the little kid says, "Nope." The guy says, "Well, where is she?" The little kid says, "Oh, she's out in the backyard, fucking the goat." They guy goes, "Oh, my God! Isn't she afraid of getting pregnant?" The little kid says, "Naaa-aaa!"

* * *

What's twelve inches long and white?
    Nothing.

* * *

Do you know why little girls carry a fish in each pocket?
    So they can smell like big girls.

* * *

This flasher is running rampant in L.A., and he comes upon three old ladies sitting on a park bench. So he flashes the first one and she has a stroke. He flashes the second one and she has a stroke. Then he flashes the third one . . . but she can't reach.

* * *

This man walks up to a bar and says, "Give me twelve shots. I'm celebrating my first blow-job." Another man leans over and says, "And I want to buy you a shot, buddy," and the first guy says, "If twelve shots can't wash the taste away, I'm sure another won't help."

Why do women have more trouble with hemorrhoids than men?

Because God made man the perfect asshole!

* * *

A Catholic missionary priest goes into the jungle to teach the Indians English and religion. The first day he's there, he gathers all the natives together, and for their first lesson, he walks over to a tepee, points at it and says, "This is a TEPEE!" And the Indians all repeat in unison, "Tepee!" Next he walks over to a tree, pats it and says, "This is a TREE!" And all the Indians say, "Tree!" Next he goes over to a fire and says, "This is a FIRE!" And all the Indians say, "Fire!" Next he goes over to a bush, shakes it and says, "This is a BUSH!" And all the Indians say, "Bush!" As he shakes the bush, however, he exposes a young Indian squaw and a brave behind the bush who are having sex. The priest is upset and flustered and doesn't know what to do, but everyone is looking at him so he points to the couple and says, "That's a BOY riding a BICYCLE!" And all the Indians say, "Bicycle!" But one Indian comes running up with a bow and arrow, and shoots one arrow into the brave! Then he shoots another arrow right into the girl! The priest turns to him in horror and says, "What are you doing!" And the Indian says, "Boy riding MY bicycle!"

* * *

A young Irish lad goes into the confessional, and he says, "Bless me, Father, for I have sinned." And the priest says, "What are your sins, my son?" "Well, Father, I've committed adultery." "Tell me the name of the young lady, my son." "Well, Father, I cannot divulge that information." "My boy," says the priest, "was it Mrs. Flanagan? Word has it that she's been out and about town these days." But the boy says, "No, Father, it wasn't Mrs. Flanagan." "Well, was it Mrs. O'Connor? She's had a roving eye!" But the boy says, "No, Father, it wasn't Mrs. O'Connor." "Well then, sure and it must be Mrs. O'Reilly. She hasn't been getting along well with her husband these days." But the boy says, "No, Father, it wasn't Mrs. O'Reilly." So the priest says, "But my boy, if you don't tell me, I cannot give you absolution!" "Well, that's okay, Father," says the boy. "You've given me three new leads!"

* * *

What do Jimmy Carter and the Long Island Rail Road have in common?

They both pulled out of Roslyn in time!

* * *

A guy is in a bar, has a few drinks with a girl and decides to take her home. So they go back to his house, and they're going to get it on, and he starts to undress. He takes his shoes and socks off, and the girl notices that his toes are all curled. So she says, "What happened to your toes?" And the guy says, "Oh, when I was young I had 'tolio.'" And she says, "Tolio? You mean Polio." And he says, "Nope. Tolio."

And he takes his pants off, and the girl notices that his knees are all twisted and bent. And she says, "What happened to your knees?" And he says, "Well, when I was real young, I had 'kneesles.'" And she says, "Kneesles! You mean Measles." And the guy says, "No, no. I mean kneesles." Then he takes his underpants off, and the girl looks at him and says, "Oh sure. Now you're going to tell me you once had SMALL COX!"

* * *

Why did God invent women?
　Because sheep can't cook!

* * *

What's the best thing to come out of a dick?
　The wrinkles!

* * *

A guy is sitting at home watching television, and runs out of cigarettes. He says to his wife, "I'm going to run down to the bar and get a pack of cigarettes. I'll be right back." So he goes down to the bar and while he's there he decides to have a drink. So he sits at the bar and has a drink. There's an attractive lady next to him, and he gets into a conversation with her. Next thing you know, they've had a few drinks and gotten a little drunk, and she invites him back to her house. So they go back to her house and have sex. Then the guy looks at his watch and says, "Oh my God! It's twelve-thirty — I'm late! I gotta get out of here!" So he jumps out of bed, gets dressed, runs to the door — stops, runs back to the girl and says, "Hey, do you have any talcum powder?" The girl says, "Yeah. Why?" He says, "Do me a favor; sprinkle a little talcum powder all over my hands." So she sprinkles the powder all over his hands, and he runs out the door and runs home.

Sure enough, he gets to his house and his wife is real upset. She yells, "Where the hell have you been!" And the guy says, "Well, I went down to the bar to buy some cigarettes, and I met this girl there and we had a few drinks. Then I went back to her house with her and we had sex." The woman says, "Don't lie to me — I see that talcum powder on your hands! You were out bowling with the boys!"

* * *

What's the fourth biggest lie?
   It's only a cold sore!

* * *

Why did God create man?
   Because you can't teach an electric vibrator to mow the lawn!

* * *

Definition of a woman:
   An attachment you screw on the bed to get the housework done!

* * *

What's the definition of virginity?
   A big issue over a little tissue!

* * *

What do women and ovens have in common?
   They both need to be hot before you stick your meat in!

* * *

Did you hear about the eighty-five-year-old man who was accused of rape?

They had to dismiss the case because the evidence against him wouldn't hold up in court!

* * *

A man and a sheep and a dog were standing on an island in the middle of nowhere. The man had been stranded there for so long that he was getting very very horny, and he kept thinking about having sex with the sheep. He finally approached the sheep and was about to mount it, but at the precise moment that he was about to consummate the act the dog came up and bit him on the ass. He couldn't believe it! A couple of weeks passed, and he thought about having sex with the sheep again, and he got it on with the sheep, and again at the precise moment that he was about to consummate it, the dog bit him on the ass. Every time he tried to have sex with the sheep, the dog bit him.

One day he saw a raft approaching the island with a beautiful, voluptuous blonde woman on it, and after landing on the island, she said, "Boy, am I happy to see you! I never thought I'd see a human being again!" The man replied, "You don't know how happy I am to see you too. I haven't had sex in months!" The woman said, "What can I do to help you out?" The man said, "Would you please hold the dog?"

* * *

A husband comes home one night after work and announces to his wife, "Darling, I've brought home some ice cream. Do you want me to dish it out?" The wife answers from the living room, "How hard is it?" The husband replies, "Oh, about as hard as my cock when you turn me on." The wife then remarks, "Well, if that's the case, pour mine into a glass!"

* * *

Why can't a honeymoon last more than six days?
Because seven days makes a hole weak!

* * *

What's the definition of vasectomy?
Our research tells us that vasectomy means never having to say you're sorry!

* * *

How does a man make love to a really ugly woman?
He does it in his hand, and then he throws it at her!

* * *

There's this elephant walking through the woods, and she steps on a nail, and a mouse comes by. The mouse pulls out the nail, and the elephant says "Thank you so much! How can I repay you?" The mouse says, "Hey, baby, it's been a long time. Let's go for it." So the elephant says, "Okay, if that's what you want — climb on." So the mouse climbs on and he's back there, pounding away, and the elephant thinks, "Jeez, this is terrible." Just then the wind kicks up and knocks down a big branch which falls and hits the elephant on the head, and she goes, "Ouch!" And the mouse says, "Yeah! Take it, bitch!"

* * *

Did you ever hear the expression that when two's company, the result is three?

There's this girl who has the largest pussy in the world. She meets a guy, a Texan, in a bar and she says, "Tex, I got the biggest hole in the world! Why don't you get your biggest cowboy boots and come up to my room with me?" So the Texan goes to her room, and he's got his big cowboy hat on, and he's got his two big boots in his hands, and he says, "These are size 13 EEE. I bet you can't get the big toe of one of these fuckers up there!" So she says, "Try me, Tex." And she lies down on the bed, spreads her legs high up in the air, and the Texan brings up his big boot. He slides the whole thing right in, and he says, "Oh, my God, we got a big one here." He takes the other boot and pushes it in a little bit, and the whole thing slides right in! The woman says, "Tex, I didn't even *feel* that!" So Tex says, "Well, try this." So he bends over and sticks his whole head in, and before he knows it he's got one shoulder in, and he falls inside her pussy! So he's inside her pussy, groping around, and he brings out his flashlight and looks around, and he sees there's another guy in there with him! Tex says, "Hey! What are *you* doing in here!" And the guy says, "I got in here the same way you did!" So Tex says, "Well, it's a good thing I got this flashlight so we can find our way out of here." The other guy says, "Let's look around a little first. If we find my car keys, we can *drive* out of here!"

* * *

A man goes to a doctor and says, "Doctor, I'm having a little problem with my penis, and I'd like you to take a look at it." So the doctor says okay, and checks it out. To the doctor's amazement, he sees that on the man's penis he has tattooed "TINY." The doctor is so astounded that he has to excuse himself, and he goes out and tells his nurse. The nurse is a voluptuous blonde woman, and the doctor says to her, "Nurse, you won't believe what this man has tattooed on his penis. You've got to see it for yourself — he has 'TINY' tattooed on his penis." So the nurse goes into the room with the patient and comes out a few minutes later with a great big smile on her face. She says, "You ought to look more closely, Doctor. It didn't say TINY, it said TICONDER- OGA, N.Y.!"

* * *

A ninety-year-old man was celebrating his birth- day by procuring a prostitute. Things didn't work out well, but he was happy he had done as well as he did. A few days later he had a strange feeling in his cock, and he hurried to a clinic for an examination. "Doctor," he said, "look at my cock. It's starting to ooze a little at the tip. I'm worried. I'm ninety years old and I must have a venereal disease." The doctor replied, "What are you worried about? That's not a disease. Congratulations — you're coming!"

* * *

An elephant and a mouse were travelling along, and suddenly the elephant fell into a large ditch. The elephant screamed up to the mouse, "Please, Mr. Mouse, save me!" The mouse said, "But how can I save you down there? You're so big!" The elephant said, "See that Mercedes we just passed? Go get the car and some chain; attach the chain to the car and pull me out." Sure enough, the mouse went and drove the Mercedes to the ditch, found some chain and, believe it or not, hoisted the huge elephant up out of the ditch. After the elephant thanked him, he proceeded to leave and the poor mouse slipped and fell into the very same ditch. The mouse said, "Please, Mr. Elephant, save me. I'm trapped down here just like you were. Go get the Mercedes and drive it over here and hoist me up the same way I got you out." The elephant said, "Mr. Mouse, I'm too big to get in that Mercedes." The mouse suggested another way to get him out — by lowering his dick down into the ditch for the mouse to climb up on. Well, the elephant did this, and the mouse was saved. The moral of this story is: *If you have a big dick, you don't need a Mercedes!*

* * *

A beautiful, voluptuous brunette walks into a doctor's office. The doctor eyes her and invites her into his office and suggests that she take off all her clothes, which she promptly does. The doctor immediately approaches her and gives her a big kiss on the mouth. The woman says, "What are you doing?" The doctor says, "I'm checking for tooth decay." The doctor then starts feeling the woman's breasts, and the woman says, "What are you doing?" The doctor says, "I'm checking for breast cancer." The doctor then tells the woman to lie down on the couch, and he immediately attacks her and makes mad, passionate love to her. The woman says, "What did you do that for?" The doctor says, "I was just checking for a social disease." The woman says,

"Good doctor, that's the reason I came here. I believe I have a social disease — I just don't know which one!"

* * *

Definition of marriage:
Two can live as bitter as one!
In "wedding," the "we" comes before the "I"!
Alimony: you get the billing without the cooing!

* * *

He's the friendly type — always inviting women up to his pad for Scotch and sofa!

* * *

There's this scientist who is known to be the smartest scientist in the world. He is called over to Europe for a conference, but is called back to the United States almost immediately for an emergency summit meeting. The only airplane available to leave is at an army base, so he gets on the plane with two other people: a hippie and a priest. As they are flying, they hit turbulence and the pilot gets on the loudspeaker and says, "I'm very sorry, but I cannot control this plane anymore, and we only have two parachutes. Consequently, you must decide between the three of you who will use the two parachutes." So the scientist says, "I am the best scientist in the entire world. My life has to be saved."

So he grabs the parachute, opens the hatch and jumps out. So the priest says in an Irish accent to the hippie, "I have lived a very long life. My time has come — you may take the remaining parachute." The hippie says, "We still have two chutes! The scientist thought he took a chute, but he took my knapsack!"

* * *

Bob goes into a bar, and it's so crowded that he can't sit down. He's wandering around, waiting for a seat, when he sees a fat woman, who also can't sit down. Eventually he goes up to the men at the bar and says, "What kind of gentleman are you anyway? None of you men have offered this lady a seat!" Then he turns to the woman and says, "But don't you worry, honey. As long as I have a face, you'll always have some place to sit!"

* * *

Sister Catherine is asking all the Catholic school children in fourth grade what they want to be when they grow up. Little Sheila says, "When I grow up, I want to be a prostitute!" Sister Catherine's eyes grow wide, and she barks, "What?" Sheila doesn't waver and repeats, "A prostitute!" Sister breathes a sigh of relief and says, "Thank God! I thought you said a Protestant!"

* * *

A young lady from the South was visiting New York for the first time, and she thought she knew how to get around the city using the feminine qualities that God had given her. When she got into a taxi, she thought she could wrangle herself a free ride. She waited until the driver turned around to look at her, and then she pulled up her skirt, revealing her naked pussy and spread legs.

"Driver, I'm just a poor young woman from down

South, and I was hoping that you might take this as my fare."

The taxi driver remarked, "Have you got anything smaller?"

* * *

Johnny went to the local whorehouse. Although he was happily married, he felt some of the romance had left his marriage and he desired something exotic and exciting. He told the madam, and she asked him how much money he had with him. They made a deal for $100, and she told him to go to room 10, where Georgiana would be waiting for him. He went to room 10, and all he saw was an empty room, and a duck. There had to be a mistake, so he went back to the madam. She told him that there was no mistake, that Georgiana the duck would give him the greatest lay he had ever had. Well, he decided that he had nothing to lose, so he went back to room 10 and after a short conversation with the duck, they had sex. Maybe it was the night, the need, the lust or the power of suggestion, but Georgiana, while not great looking, and even a little ugly for a duck, was a great lay. Johnny couldn't help but wonder, if Georgiana laid an egg, whether he would be its father.

The next night he went back to the same brothel and spoke to the madam. "Last night was wild!" he confessed. "But now I feel the need for something even more exciting. What do you have?" The madam was upset. "Too bad you weren't here ten minutes ago. You could have had something great in room 10. But for $100, go to room 14 on the fourth floor."

He followed her instructions and there in room 14 were six people all lying on the floor, looking through holes into the room below. Johnny looked and saw two men and two women making wild love below. "Wow, this is incredible!" he screamed. To which the man next to him replied, "This is nothing. You should have been here last night to watch some idiot fucking a duck!"

* * *

Two girls are sitting in a movie theater next to a strange-looking guy. Suddenly one woman says, "Tricia, let's get out of here. The man next to you is masturbating." Tricia says, "I can't. He's using my hand!"

* * *

Mr. Albert James was stark naked in front of his open window, doing his morning aerobics. His wife entered the room and shouted, "Albert, you fool, draw those curtains! I don't want the neighbors to think that I married you for your money!"

* * *

Did you hear about the husband who divorced his wife because he heard that all his friends had it in for him?

* * *

A beautiful platinum blonde walks into a bar. This metallurgist sizes her up in a minute. He turns to his friend and says, "Careful, mate, she's not virgin metal." His friend asks, "What is she?" The man replies, "She's a common ore!"

"Can you believe this?" a husband laughs. "This ugly-looking janitor told me that he's made love to every woman in his building. Not only has he made love to each of them, but on his birthday every woman gave him a blow-job in the elevator! Every woman except one. He left out one, I suppose, to make it believable." "Wow," his wife exclaimed. "Poor Mrs. James from 7D was in Hawaii on vacation. She'll be disappointed, but she'll make up for it!"

* * *

A guy and a girl are out on their first date, and he really tries to impress her. He takes her out to dinner to a nice restaurant, then to a hit Broadway show, then out to New York's finest clubs, finally ending up at her place, where they make mad, passionate love. After they make love, they share a cigarette and are making small talk when he asks her, "How was everything tonight, darling?" She says, "Dinner was fantastic, the show was fabulous, dancing with you was out of this world, but quite frankly, I'm a little disappointed." Surprised, he questions, "Why?" She replies, "Well, to tell you the truth, I didn't realize your organ was so small!" To which he responds, "Honey, I didn't know I'd be playing in a cathedral!"

* * *

What's the difference between little girls and little boys?

A little girl and a little boy were playing, and the boy said to the girl, "I bet I have something that you don't have." So he pulled up his shirt and pointed to his belly button. The little girl pulled up her shirt, pointed to her own belly button and said, "Oh, no you don't!" The little boy continued, "I bet you don't have two of *these*." So he pulled up his shirt and pointed to his nipples. The little girl did the same and said, "Oh, yes I do. Here they are!" And she pointed to her own. The little boy wouldn't give up, so he pulled down his pants and pointed to his penis. The little girl pulled her pants down, naturally didn't see a penis and went home crying.

The next day the little boy saw the little girl humming and skipping along. He said to her, "What are you so happy about? You don't even have one of *these*." And he points to his penis. The little girl, now secure, pointed to her cunt and said, "My mommy says that as long as I have one of *these*, I can have as many of *those* as I want!"

* * *

A pair of newlyweds buy a new house. As they're moving in, the wife notices that the husband has a black box. She asks him what's in it, and he replies, "It's from the past, darling. I'd rather not talk about it. I ask only one thing — please don't look in it." The wife, respecting her new husband's wishes, agrees. So a year goes by, and she doesn't look in the box. Another five years pass, and she still doesn't look. After thirty years, as she's cleaning the closet, she finally looks in the box. In it she finds three golf balls and $10,000. When her husband comes home that evening, she says, "I'm sorry, dear. I was cleaning today, and I opened the black box. What's it all about?" The husband sighs and says, "Well, every time I had an affair, I put a golf ball in the box." The wife thinks a minute and says, "Only three golf balls. I guess I can forgive you." The husband still looks upset. He goes on, "Yeah, but every time I got a dozen balls, I sold them!"

* * *

What's the difference between an airplane and a penis?

As an airplane get higher, it gets smaller, and as a penis gets higher, it gets bigger!

* * *

What's the difference between a theater curtain and a woman's slip?

In the theater, when the curtain goes up, everything begins. When a woman's slip goes up, everything is over!

* * *

What's the difference between a Mafia boss and a one-inch penis?

Nothing. You can't fuck with either of them!

* * *

An incredible convention took place in Los Angeles this year for all the sex-toy manufacturers and distributors. . . . Everybody in the entire industry CAME!

* * *

A young kid is in the induction line for the Korean War. He's standing there, totally stripped, and in a fit of panic he screams, "I don't want to go to Korea! I don't want to go to Korea!" He runs out of the recruiting center, naked as can be, still screaming, "I don't want to go to Korea! I don't want to go to Korea!" In a flash the two MPs from the center are in hot pursuit. Desperate, the kid sees a nun standing on a corner and says to her, "Please, Sister, I'm not crazy. I just don't want to go to Korea. Can I hide under your habit?" The nun agrees, just as the MPs approach. One asks, "Sister, have you seen a naked man running down the street screaming?" The nun nods and points down the street, and the MPs take off. When they're out of sight, she gives the young man a signal, and he crawls out. He says, "Thanks, Sister, you've saved my life. And by the way, when I was under your habit, I looked up. You've got a great pair of legs." The nun replies, "That's nothing. If you looked up a little further, you'd have seen a pair of balls! You see, I don't want to go to Korea either!"

* * *

What's the difference between snowboys and snowgirls?
   SNOWBALLS!

* * *

A pair of newlyweds go on a honeymoon to Jamaica. While sitting poolside, the husband suddenly jumps in the water and starts swimming laps. He does hundreds of laps, with a beautiful stroke, very fast. The wife notices his speed and form and says, "Honey, that's wonderful! Where'd you learn to swim like that?" The husband replies humbly, "That's in the past, honey. I'd rather not talk about it." The wife is so amazed she won't let up. "Come on, darling, you're great!" He finally says, "You may as well know, I worked very hard to swim like that. I was an Olympic swimmer." The wife smiles with respect. Pretty soon she jumps in the pool and starts swimming lap after lap, as fast as she can. Everyone is watching in amazement. When the wife finishes, the husband asks her the same question. She also says, "That's in the past, honey. I'd rather not talk about it." The husband has to find out, so he pushes her to answer. She replies, "Well, you might as well know, I worked very hard to swim like that. I was a streetwalker in Venice!"

The Worst Diet You Ever Ate

Two cannibals kill a missionary. They argue for a while about how to divide him up, and finally one of them says, "Okay. You start at the head and I'll start at the feet." So they begin their feast. After a while one of them says, "Hey, this is really great. I'm having a ball." "Slow down!" cries the other cannibal. "You're eating too fast!"

* * *

A little boy and his father are walking in the park when the boy sees a honeybee and steps on it and kills it. The father says, "Oh, for killing that honeybee you're not going to have any honey for the rest of your life." So they're walking along a little bit more, and the little boy goes over and tramples a buttercup. His father says, "Oh, for trampling that buttercup, you're not going to have any butter for the rest of the year." So finally they go home, and the little boy's mother is preparing supper, and they're waiting for the supper at the table, and the mother sees a cockroach crawling across the table, so she kills it. The little boy then looks up at his father and says, "Should I tell her, Dad, or should you?!"

* * *

A man is in a bar and all of a sudden he sees a beautiful Chinese woman who winks at him from the end of the bar. He says to the bartender, "Send that woman a drink." So the woman accepts the drink and then comes over to him and says, "Hey, mister, would you like to come up to my room with me?" The man says yes. So they go up to her room and get undressed, and they're in bed together when all of a sudden the Chinese woman pulls out a gun and puts it to his head, and she says, "Eat me mister!" So the guy says, "Okay!" And he proceeds to perform oral sex on this Chinese woman, who is a total stranger. So he does this and then leaves. Next day, same time, he goes back to the same bar and he tells the bartender the story. The Chinese woman walks in and looks at the guy and smiles. So the guy says to the bartender, "Send that woman another drink." And the bartender says "What! After what she did to you?" And the guy says, "Yeah. Chinese food doesn't stick with you very long!"

* * *

A drunk staggers into a diner and orders a couple of eggs. The waiter, suspecting that they've run out, goes back to question the chef. "Hey, Vito, do we have any more eggs?" Vito replies, "No, I don't have any fresh eggs, but I've got two rotten eggs." So the waiter replies, "Give him the rotten eggs; he's so bombed that he won't know the difference." Vito prepares the rotten eggs with a heap of fried potatoes, toast, coffee — the works. The drunk is so hungry he wolfs down the breakfast without comment. When he's ready to leave, he's at the cashier, and he asks, "Where'd you get those eggs?" She replies, "We have our own chicken farm." The drunk asks, "Do you have a rooster?" The cashier answers, "No." The drunk replies, "Well, you'd better get one, because some skunk is screwing your chickens."

* * *

Father, you don't have to wait for the shrimp boats because my brother is coming home with the crabs!

* * *

What's white and crawls up your ass?
Uncle Ben's Perverted Rice!
What's black and crawls up a girl's ass?
Uncle Ben!

* * *

A woman was married three different times and was still a virgin! Her first husband was a psychologist and he liked to talk about it, her second husband was a gynecologist and he liked to look at it, and her third husband was a gourmet!

* * *

A man goes into a hamburger stand and orders a burger. The waitress takes out two frozen patties and sticks them under her arms. The man says, "What are you doing?" She replies, "I'm defrosting them!" The other guy at the counter says, "In that case, you can cancel my fucking hot dog!"

Hollyweird!

What's blue and sings alone?
  Dan Aykroyd!

* * *

What's the difference between a moose and Guy Lombardo's Orchestra?
  With a moose, the horns are in front and the asshole's in the rear!

* * *

Did you hear about the new law in California where you're not allowed to use rats anymore for laboratory testing?
Instead they're going to use lawyers! After all, there are more lawyers than rats, you don't get as attached to lawyers as you do to rats, and you can get lawyers to do things that a rat would never do!

Did you hear about the new Jewish porno movie?
  Debby Does Nothing!

* * *

This beautiful young woman has three suitors, all
of whom want to marry her. So she sets up a contest
and says, "You all have three years to complete this
quest: I'll marry the man who brings me the most
Ping-Pong balls." The men all set out on the quest,
and after about a year, the first man returns with
a vanload of Ping-Pong balls. The woman says, "Just
one van full? I'm sorry, we'll have to wait for the
other two men." Another year passes, and the second
guy returns with a trainload of Ping-Pong balls. The
woman is pretty impressed, but she still says they
have to wait until all three men have had a chance.
The three-year deadline is almost over, right down
to the last minutes, and they see the third guy coming
over the hill, all tattered and bloody, carrying a sack.
When the woman sees him she says, "Is this what
I waited for? In three years is this all the Ping-Pong
balls you could find?" And the third guy says, "PING-
PONG BALLS??!! I thought you said 'KING
KONG'S BALLS!'"

* * *

Los Angeles is so strange.... Did you hear about
the two judges who tried each other?

* * *

What has more fingerprints, the FBI or the ETA?
What's the ETA?
Elizabeth Taylor's Ass!

Business at the theater was so bad the doormen got arrested for loitering!

* * *

A little Jewish tailor in Hollywood has a client who comes in and wants a suit made for him. When he comes in the first day, he takes the guy's measurements. The second day the guy comes around and finds that the suit is not ready. The little Jewish guy doesn't want to alienate his customer, so he invites him to lunch to talk about the suit.

So they go to a nice restaurant, and while they're sitting down and having a bite to eat, the little Jewish guy sees a celebrity going into the bathroom. So he excuses himself and goes into the bathroom. Sure enough, it is Bernie Schwartz. So he says, "Bernie, listen. I'm a little Jewish tailor here in Los Angeles, and I have an important client with me. I'm going to make him a few suits. Could you do me a big favor? Could you please come over to my table, and when you get there could you just say, 'Hi there, Hymie, how are you? And by the way Hymie, how are my suits making out?' I'd really appreciate it." So the little Jewish guy goes back to his table and starts talking to his client. Bernie walks over to them, just as planned, and he says, "Hymie! How are you? How are my suits making out?" Hymie turns to him and says, "Friggin' Bernie, leave me alone — can't you see I'm busy!"

* * *

The Hollywood starlet had her legs insured for $1 million . . . .And that was just for theft!

What has two cherries and dances?
One hundred Las Vegas dancers!

* * *

The owner of the new theatre said business was so bad that he'd looked at more empty seats than a tailor!

Ethnic Jokes

Black Jokes

A country club owner is in Japan on business, and while he's there he decides to play a round of golf. So he goes to the country club and goes out on the course, and he immediately notices that the course is in perfect condition. The greens are like velvet, the fairways are immaculate, the trees are cut to perfection. When he gets back to the clubhouse after playing his round, he goes to see the manager and says, "This is the most beautiful course I have ever seen in my life. How do you do it?" And the manager says, "It's simple — we use robots. Didn't you see any out there? They work every day, rain or shine, they never get tired, and they do exactly what they're told." "Fantastic!" says the American. "Listen, do you think I could take any home with me?"

48

So they work out a deal, and the American buys a dozen robots to put to work at his own country club. Two months go by, and the guy is ecstatic. His course is beautiful: every blade of grass is cut to the same height, the water hazards are clear and sparkling. Everything is great, in fact, except for one thing. When the sun is high in the sky, sometimes it glances off the robot's metal bodies and throws light in the golfers' eyes. He's gotten one or two complaints about this, so he decides to call Japan. The manager in Japan is a little surprised at the complaint, but he says, "Well, tell you what. Why don't you paint the robots black? That way no sun will reflect off them." The American manager thinks this is a great idea, so he has all twelve robots painted black that very day. The next day, only two out of twelve robots show up for work!

* * *

Two black guys are out fishing one day on the Mississippi River, and one man says to the other, "Hey, Jeremiah, pull your pecker out and let it down into the water and let me know if the water's cold." Jeremiah says, "Okay," and proceeds to do this, and his friend says, "Well, is it cold?" And Jeremiah says, "No . . . but it sure is deep!"

* * *

What is black, has white eyes and knocks on glass?
A black in a microwave!

* * *

Why don't blacks like blow-jobs?
They don't like any job!

What do you call a black Smurf?
  A smigger!

* * *

Why does Georgia have blacks and California have earthquakes?
  California had first pick!

* * *

What do you call a black lady with braces?
  Black and Decker Pecker Wrecker!

* * *

What's the definition of endless love?
  Stevie Wonder and Ray Charles playing tennis!

* * *

What's the difference between a women's track team and a tribe of smart pygmies?
  The pygmies are a pack of cunning runts and the track team is a pack of running cunts!

* * *

What do you get when you cross a black and an Irishman?
  A leprecoon!

* * *

Why do blacks keep their flies open?
  In case they want to count to eleven!

* * *

What do you call a black man in Thailand?
  A tycoon!

Why did God invent golf?
So that white people could dress up like black people!

* * *

How do you solve the Puerto Rican problem?
Tell the blacks they taste like fried chicken!

* * *

What's the definition of worthless?
A seven-foot-two-inch black with a small cock who can't play basketball!

* * *

What do you get when you cross a black and a groundhog?
Six more weeks of basketball season!

* * *

How do you know Adam and Eve were not black?
Ever try to take a rib away from a black man?

* * *

Did you hear about the little black kid who had diarrhea?
He thought he was melting!

* * *

What do they call a woman in the army?
A WAC.
What do they call a black woman in the army?
A WACOON!

* * *

Why do blacks always have sex on their minds?
Because of the pubic hair on their heads!

Did you hear about the new black French restaurant?
  Chez What?!

* * *

What's black and shines in the dark?
  Oakland!

* * *

What did Lincoln say after his five-day drunk?
  "I freed WHO?"

* * *

Why don't blacks and Hispanics marry?
  Because their kids would be too lazy to steal!

* * *

How come God gave black people soul?
  Because he fucked up in the hair department!

* * *

If you throw a black person and a log off a cliff,
which one lands first?
  Who cares!

* * *

Three black girls are sitting around talking about
their boyfriends, and one says, "I calls my boyfriend
'86' because he's eight inches long and six inches
around." The next girl says, "I calls my boyfriend
'27' because he's two times a day, seven times a week."
The last girl says, "I calls my boyfriend 'Drambuie.'"
And the others ask, "Why you call him Drambuie?
That sound like a liquor." And the last girl says,
"That's him!"

A black man and his wife are having trouble having babies, and they try and they try with no luck. So they go to the doctor to see what he has to say. The man goes in and the doctor looks at him, and the doctor says, "I'm sorry, but you're impotent." The guy says, "What's that?" And the doctor says, "Well, you can't have babies!" So the black guy goes out, buys this big pink Cadillac and this big hat with a feather on it, and he drives home. His wife says, "What the hell you got that big hat with the feather on it, and that big pink car?" And the guy says, "Well, I went to the doctor, and he said you can't have babies because I'm impotent. And if I'm gonna be impotent, I'm gonna *look* impotent!"

* * *

One day a black Supreme Court judge went out with the boys at lunch and got rip-roaring drunk. He vomited all over himself, staggered home and fell down on the couch. Along came his wife, who took one look at him and said, "Amos! What in the hell's going on? You have vomit all over yourself! What's wrong with you?" And Amos rolled over and said, "What? I didn't do this! I was on the bus and this drunk came up to me and lost it all over me! But don't you worry — we arrested him, and I'm gonna give that sucker thirty days!" So she told him to get out of the clothes. He showered, put himself back together and went back to work. Pretty soon the phone rang and Amos answered it just before he came out of his chambers, and it was his wife. She said, "Amos, what about that man you caught?" Amos said, "I've got him right here in front

of me. Don't worry, I'm gonna give him sixty days!"
She said, "You'd better give him ninety days, 'cause
he shit in your pants too!"

* * *

Did you hear that the NFL is painting all the
footballs green this year for the Super Bowl? After
all, when was the last time you saw a black drop
a watermelon!

Gay Jokes

Two gay guys were standing on the Golden Gate Bridge, and one of them said, "What's that?" And the other gay said, "That's the Sausalito ferry boat." "Wow," said the first guy. "I knew we were organized, but I didn't know we had our own navy!"

* * *

What does GAY stand for?
  "Got AIDS Yet!"

* * *

Did you hear that the Statue of Liberty has AIDS?
  We think it caught it from one of the ferry boats!

* * *

The mohels collect all the foreskins, but then what do they do with them?
  They sell them to homosexuals for chewing gum!

What's the difference between beer nuts, and deer nuts?

Beer nuts are a buck and a half, deer nuts are under a buck!

* * *

What do you get when you cross a gay Eskimo and a black?

A snowblower that doesn't work!

* * *

What's the definition of a real buddy?

Someone who'll go down and get two blow-jobs and come back and give you one!

* * *

What's organic dental floss?

Pubic hair!

* * *

In Greece, how do they separate the men from the boys?

With a crowbar!

* * *

What do gay men refer to hemorrhoids as?

Speed bumps!

* * *

What's the hardest part about AIDS?

Leaving your friends behind!

* * *

What's the difference between a gay rodeo and a straight rodeo?

At a straight rodeo they yell, "Ride that sucker!"
At a gay rodeo they yell, "Suck that rider!"

* * *

A German approaches a bar at eight o'clock in the morning and starts banging at the doors and windows, begging to be let in for a drink. The bartender, who's cleaning up, hollers, "We're closed. We're closed!" The German says, "Please, please, I've got to have a drink, I just found out my brother's a homo!" So the bartender lets him in, and he has his drink. A couple of weeks pass, and the same German appears at the bar again at eight o'clock in the morning, banging away at the door, and says, "Let me in, let me in! I found out my twin brother is gay!" The bartender lets him in again, the guy has his drink and goes. Two more weeks pass, and the same guy shows up again at eight A.M., and the bartender, who's pretty tired of this routine, says, "Wait a minute, buddy, don't you have anybody in your family who likes pussy?" The German says, "Yeah, that's why I'm here! I just found out that it's my sister!"

* * *

What does AIDS stand for?
Anally Induced Death Sentence!

* * *

Two gay men are talking when one says to the other, "Sex is a pain in the ass!" The other one looks at him and says, "You must be doing it wrong!"

How does a gay person tell an old man from a young boy in the dark?
It's not hard!

* * *

Typical gay birthday card:
You're 9½ inches....
I find that hard to swallow!

* * *

A man and his lady are fucking in the back seat of a car. All of a sudden a cop shines a flashlight on them. He says,"Alright, I'm taking you in." The man says, "Please, officer, give me a break. I'll do anything." The cop says "Alright, I'm next!" The man says, "But I've never fucked a cop before!"

* * *

What does a gay person call a condom?
Seal-a-meal!

* * *

Did you hear about the two gay reindeer?
They said, "Let's go down to the Elk's Club and blow some bucks!"

* * *

What does AIDS really stand for?
Another Idiotic Dick Sucker!

* * *

Misery is finding out that your son has gone into law enforcement....as a meter maid!

A sign in a San Francisco bar reads
CALL BEAUTIFUL BLONDE AT 444-1294.
If a man answers it's ME!

* * *

Rest room sign in the Village:
HIS — HERS — Let your conscience be your guide!

* * *

EXXON put a queer tiger in his tank and it blew the engine!

* * *

Sign in a Christopher Street bar reads:
GUESS YOUR SEX — $1

* * *

Love is a many gendered thing!

* * *

Did you hear about the gay fellow who redecorated his bathroom and has HIS and HIS towels?

* * *

Gay man's motto:
I kiss every man I please, and I please every man I kiss!

Italian Jokes

What is the shortest book ever written?
Italian War Heroes.

* * *

Two Italians are walking down the street. They cross paths and stop dead in their tracks. One turns to the other and says, "Oh my God! You look exactly like me!" Sure enough, they look exactly alike and they're dressed just the same. So one says to the other, "Whatsa you name?" The guy says, "Giuseppe LaRosa!" The first guy says, "Oh my God! Thatsa my name too! Where were you born?" The other guy goes, "I was born in Palermo, Sicily, in Italy." The first guy says, "Oh my God, I was born in Palermo too! What's you mama's name?" The guy says, "My mamma's Rosa. What's you mama's name?" The first guy says, "Oh my God! My mamma's a Rosa too. Somethin' here is-a very wrong!" So one says to the other, "Wait a second! Here's a piece-a chalk. You write your name on the wall, and I write my name on the wall, and we compare the signatures!" So the first one writes two big X's, and the second one writes two big X's and then down at the bottom two little x's. The two guys look at the signatures and one says, "Thank God, no problem! You're Giuseppe LaRosa, and I'm-a Giuseppe LaRosa, M.D!"

* * *

What's red, green, blue, yellow, purple and orange?
   An Italian all dressed up!

* * *

What do you call an Italian who marries a black?
   A social climber!

* * *

What do you get when you cross a Mexican and an Italian?
   A guy who makes you an offer you can't understand!

* * *

Why do Italian men have mustaches?
   So they can look like their mothers!

* * *

Why do Puerto Ricans throw away their garbage in clear plastic bags?
   So Italians can go window shopping!

Did you hear about the Italian who broke his nose open to see what made it run?

* * *

An Italian flyer is shot down over Poland. The Italian is placed in a hospital and has his leg amputated. When he sees a Polish flyer walking by, the Italian asks him to drop his leg over his native land. The Polish flyer, in the spirit of camaraderie, agrees. Later the Italian has his arm amputated and asks the Pole to drop it over Italy. Then the Italian has his other leg amputated and asks the Pole to drop it over Italy. This time the Pole eyes the Italian suspiciously and asks, "What are you trying to do, escape?"

* * *

Why are so many Italian men in this country named Tony?

Because when they got to Ellis Island, they were all stamped "TO N.Y."

Jewish Jokes

A ninety-year-old Jewish couple decide to get a divorce. They go to the judge and say, "Judge, we want a divorce." The judge says, "You've been married fifty years and now you want to get a divorce? Why did you wait so long?" And the couple says, "Well, we wanted to wait until the kids were dead!"

* * *

A Jew and a Czech are camping together in the wilds in Canada when suddenly two bears appear. Before they can run away, one of the bears grabs the Czech. The Jew, terrified, makes his escape and runs like mad. He finds a Mountie, tells him the story, and the two of them hurry back to camp. When they get there, the two bears, a male and a female, are still sitting there, but the Czech is gone.

The Mountie says, "Which one of them ate the Czech?" "That one," says the Jew, "the male." So the Mountie shoots the male bear, but when they cut him open his stomach is empty. What is the moral of this story?

Never trust a Jew who says the Czech is in the male!

* * *

What's the difference between a JAP and a toilet?

A toilet doesn't follow you around for nine months after you use it!

* * *

How was the Grand Canyon formed?

A Jew dropped a nickel down a gopher hole!

* * *

One day Sol and Izzie, two diamond dealers, meet on Forty-seventh street, and Sol says, "Izzie! You have any diamonds for sale?" Izzie says "I just happen to have a diamond here." Sol says, "What do you want for it?" Izzie says, "Give me $1,000." So Sol gives Izzie $1,000 and takes the diamond. A couple of days later they meet on the street and Izzie says, "Sol, do you have that diamond I sold you the other day?" Sol says, "Yeah." Izzie says, "What do you want for it?" Sol says, "Oh, give me $2,000." So he gives Sol $2,000 and takes the diamond. A couple of days later they meet again, and Sol says to Izzie, "Izzie! Do you have that diamond I sold you?" And Izzie says, "Yeah." Sol says, "How much do you want for it?" Izzie says, "$3,000." Sol pays him the $3,000 and takes the diamond. A few days later they meet again on the street. Izzie says, "Sol do you have that diamond?" And Sol says, "Nah! I sold it." Izzie says, "Why did you do that! We were making a good living on that diamond!"

* * *

What's a JAP's idea of perfect sex?
  Simultaneous headaches!

* * *

What do you get when you cross a Jew with a Gypsy?
  A chain of empty stores!

* * *

What do you get when you cross a Jewish American Princess and a computer?
  A computer that never goes down on you!

* * *

What's a JAP's favorite wine?
  I wanna go to Palm Springs!

* * *

How does a JAP do it doggy style?
  She makes him beg for an hour and then rolls over and plays dead!

* * *

How was copper wire invented?
  From Jews fighting over a penny!

* * *

What do you call a Jewish woman's water bed?
  The Dead Sea!

Did you hear about the new brand of Jewish tires — Firestein?

They not only stop on a dime, they pick it up!

* * *

What's the difference between a Jewish mother and a vulture?

A vulture waits till you're dead to eat your heart out!

* * *

What's the difference between circumcision and crucifixion?

In a crucifixion, they throw out the whole Jew!

* * *

What's a JAP's idea of natural childbirth?

Absolutely no makeup.

* * *

Why do JAPs close their eyes while they're screwing?

So they can pretend they're shopping!

* * *

What does a JAP do during a nuclear holocaust?

Gets out her sun reflector!

* * *

What's Jewish foreplay?

Twenty minutes of begging!

* * *

How do you know when a JAP has an orgasm?

She drops her nail file!

Why do JAPs like to use fourteen-carat-gold diaphragms?

Because they like their husbands to come into money!

* * *

What does a JAP do with her asshole?

Dresses him up in a suit and sends him off to work!

* * *

Did you hear about the rabbi who committed suicide?

He found out the girl he was eating was a pig!

* * *

Why do Jewish men die before their wives do?

Because they want to!

* * *

How did they finally prove that Jesus Christ was Jewish?

He lived at home until he was thirty, he worked in his father's business, and his mother thought he was God!

Mexican Jokes

Did you hear about the two Mexicans on "That's Incredible"?

One had auto insurance, and one was an only child!

* * *

What's six miles long and goes four miles per hour?

A Mexican funeral with only one set of jumper cables!

* * *

Why do Mexicans have noses?

So they have something to pick in the winter!

* * *

What do you call a Mexican with a vasectomy?

A dry Martinez!

Why do Mexican women wear long skirts?
  To hide the No-Pest strips!

* * *

How many Mexicans does it take to grease a car?
  One, if you hit him right!

* * *

A Mexican kid gets his first razor on his sixteenth birthday, and he's so excited he doesn't know whether to shave first or slash tires!

* * *

I knew this Mexican who ran for mayor, and made it. He ran for governor, and made it. He ran for Presidente, and made it. He ran for the border ... and didn't make it!

* * *

Did you hear about the Mexican janitor who got fired from his job cleaning toilets in a Las Vegas hotel?
  They found him skimming off the top!

Polish Jokes

Did you hear about the Polack who was found dead in his jail cell with twelve bumps on his head?
    He tried to hang himself with a rubber band!

* * *

Why don't they let Polacks swim in the ocean?
    Because they leave a ring!

* * *

Why does the new Polish Navy have glass-bottomed boats?
    So they can see the old Polish Navy!

* * *

Why don't they give Polish work crews more than half an hour for lunch?
    They don't want to retrain them!

Why don't they use the 911 system in Poland?

Polacks can't find the 11 on the telephone dial!

* * *

What do Polish women do when they are done sucking cock?

Spit out the feathers!

* * *

Why do they paint the garbage cans orange in Poland?

So the Polacks will think they are eating at Howard Johnson's!

* * *

Do you know what the definition of gross ignorance is?

One hundred forty-four Polacks!

* * *

Did you hear about the Polack who had a penis implant?

His hand rejected it!

* * *

A Polack has a parking lot with a sign outside: "OPEN TWENTY-FOUR HOURS!" A man comes up and sees that the lot is closed, and says, "Your sign says 'Open twenty-four hours.' Why are you closed?" The Polack says, "We are open twenty-fours hours....but not in a row!"

* * *

Did you hear the one about the cardinal who went up to the Pope and said, "Would you like to hear a Polish joke?" And the Pope said, "Yes, I would, but of course you know that I'm Polish." And the cardinal said, "Yes, I know that. That's why I'm going to tell the joke very s-l-o-w-l-y."

* * *

A guy decides to have a beer in his local bar, so he goes in and orders a beer and he's sitting there drinking it. After a while he needs to pee, so he goes into the bathroom and is standing at a urinal, and a black man comes in and stands at the urinal next to him. When the guy looks down, he happens to see that the black man's penis is snow white! He can't believe it! So he zips up his pants and goes out to the bar and he says, "Hey, Charlie! You won't believe what I just saw." Charlie says, "Well, what did you see?" So the guy says, "Well, I was in the john taking a leak when I looked at this black guy standing next to me at the urinal. I looked down and he had a white penis! I mean, it was snow white!" Charlie says, "Oh, that's not a black guy. That's just a Polish coal miner back from his honeymoon!"

* * *

Did you hear about the Polish ice hockey team?
    They all drowned during spring training!

* * *

How many Polacks does it take to go ice fishing?
    Three. One to cut a hole in the ice, and two to push the boat through it.

* * *

Did you hear about the Polish ice fisherman's wife?
    He brought home five hundred pounds of ice, and she drowned cooking it.

Did you hear about the Polish bank robber?
  He tied up the safe and blew up the guard.

* * *

Did you hear about the Polish kamikaze planes?
  They had seating for eight!

* * *

How do you ruin a Polish party?
  Flush the punch bowl!

* * *

What do you get when you cross a Polack and a Chicano?
  A kid who spray-paints his name on chain-link fences!

* * *

Why do they play on artificial turf in Poland?
  To keep the cheerleaders from grazing!

* * *

Who won the race down the tunnel, the black or the Pole?
  The Pole, because the black had to stop and write "MOTHERFUCKER" on the wall!

* * *

Did you hear about the Polish abortion clinic?
  There's a yearlong waiting list!

* * *

What's green and flies over Poland?
  Peter Panski!

Did you hear about the Pole who went out and bought four snow tires?

They melted on the way home!

* * *

Did you hear about the Pole who lost $50 on the football game?

He lost $25 for the game, and $25 on the instant replay!

* * *

What do you call a Pole with 1,500 girlfriends?

A shepherd!

* * *

Why did the Polack snort Nutra-Sweet?

He thought it was Diet Coke!

* * *

Did you hear about the Polack who locked his keys in the car?

He went and got a coat hanger to get his family out!

* * *

Did you hear about the Polack who thought that a sanitary belt was a drink in a clean glass!

* * *

Did you hear about the Polack who was with his girlfriend in a farmer's field, and she got cold?

He got up and closed the gate!

* * *

A guy walks into a bar and says to the bartender, "I've got a terrific Polish joke to tell you." The bartender says, "Hey, wait a minute. I'm six foot four, and I'm a former football player. I was a line backer, I know karate and I'm Polish, so be careful. And you see that guy next to you? He's six foot two; he was a wrestler who won the World Collegiate Wrestling Championship. He's of Polish descent too, so be careful. The other guy sitting on the other side of you was a former boxer, a Golden Gloves champion who comes from Pittsburgh, Pennsylvania. So be careful what you're saying, I'm just warning you!" The guy says, "I'm tired already, I've lost my patience. I'd have to explain it three times!"

* * *

Did you hear about the Polack who put iodine on his paycheck because he got a cut in pay!

* * *

Did you hear about how the Polish Army lost the war?
    They deserted!

* * *

Did you hear about how the Russians invaded Poland?
    They walked in backward and told them they were leaving!

* * *

Did you hear about how the Polacks got to America?
    One swam over and the others walked over on his scum!

How do you contract Polish AIDS?
  Kissing!

* * *

What do you call a Polack who can spell "cat"?
  Gifted!

* * *

Did you hear about the Polack who didn't tell his wife that he was senile until after she was pregnant?

* * *

Do you know how to get a Polack out of a bathtub?
  Fill it with water!

* * *

There's this Polish elephant trainer who will give anyone in the audience $500 if he can make his elephant kneel without touching it. So this Italian comes down from the audience carrying two bricks and slaps the elephant on the balls, and the elphant kneels. The Polish trainer pays the guy $500. So the next night the Polish trainer has been thinking about it, and decides to change his act. He says, "If there's anyone who can make my elephant say yes by nodding its head and no by shaking its head, without touching it, will get $500." So the same Italian guy comes down from the audience, walks right up to the elephant, looks him in the eye and says, "Remember me?" And the elephant nods his head up and down. Then the Italian says, "Want me to do it again?" The elephant shakes its head, and the Italian wins another $500!

An Italian, Frenchman and Polack are in the desert. The Italian has a loaf of bread, the Frenchman a bottle of wine, and the Polack has a car door. When they ask each other to explain the objects they brought, the Italian says, "If I get hungry, I can eat the bread!" The Frenchman says, "If I get thirsty, I can drink the wine!" The Polack says, "If it gets hot, I can roll down the window!

* * *

A Polish guy brings his girlfriend three dozen beautiful roses. The girlfriend is just thrilled, and she strips off her clothes, lies down on the bed and spreads her legs. The man comes into the bedroom and looks at her. She says to him, "This is for the roses." He says to her, "What's the matter, you can't find a vase?"

Miscellaneous

A traveler goes up to the airline-ticket agent and says, "I have three pieces of luggage. I want one to go to Toronto, one to go to Los Angeles and one to New York City." The agent replies, "You can't do that." "Why not?" says the traveler. "You did it last week!"

* * *

God and Moses are out playing golf. Moses swings and makes a beautiful shot, the ball making a perfect arch and landing on the green. God steps up to the tee and swings at the ball, but his shot hooks violently and disappears into the bushes. Suddenly a rabbit darts out of the bushes with the ball in his mouth. The rabbit starts running to the hole and then suddenly starts going the wrong way. An eagle swoops down, snatches up the rabbit and flies right over the green. A bolt of lightning out of nowhere strikes the eagle, the eagle drops the rabbit, the rabbit falls onto the green, drops the ball, and the ball rolls right into the cup for a hole in one. Moses turns to God and says, "Are you going to screw around or are you going to play golf?"

* * *

What do you call an Indian brave who has three balls?
A buck and a half.

* * *

A shady-looking itinerant walks into a Catholic church, goes down the aisle and catches the priest's eye. He continues walking around, all through the church, up and down the aisles, and the priest is keeping an eye on him because he looks suspicious. Finally he goes into the confessional. The priest figures, well, maybe he just wants to go to confession. So the priest goes to his side, slides open the door and says, "May I help you, my son?" And the itinerant says, "Yeah. You got any toilet paper on your side?"

* * *

What do you call an Oriental person on Quaaludes?
A mellow yellow!

* * *

Did you hear about the Indian chief who traded in his forty-year-old squaw for two twenty-year-olds? A couple of weeks later a couple of fellow braves saw him back with his forty-year-old squaw. They said, "What happened to your two twenty-year-olds?" The chief replied, "Me no wired for 220!"

* * *

An American tourist is in Scotland, and while touring the moors, she comes upon a Scotsman who got drunk the night before and passed out under a tree. She sees that the man is out cold and decides to satisfy her curiosity about what Scottish men have under their kilts. So she tiptoes over to the man, lifts up his kilt and sees for sure that the rumors are true! So she takes out a ribbon, ties it on the Scotsman and leaves. When the man wakes up, he has to pee really badly, so he goes over to the creek, lifts up his kilt, sees the ribbon and says, "I don't know what you've done or where you've been, but I'm happy you got first prize!"

* * *

What do you call a fat Chinaman?
   A Chunk!

* * *

One Puerto Rican talking to another in a New York subway:
   "Don't just stand there — spray something!"

* * *

What's the highest ideal in Greek culture?
   A young boy and a bottle of olive oil!

* * *

Did you hear about the new book on overpopulation by the noted Chinese scholar Fuk Em Yung!

What's green and has 20,000 assholes?
  The Saint Patty's Day Parade!

* * *

Did you hear about the lazy Texan who bought his wife a yacht for Christmas so he wouldn't have anything to wrap!

* * *

His ancestors never made an honest dollar... and he's following in their fingerprints!

* * *

What do you get when you cross a Frenchman with a Chinaman?
  You get a Frenchman who eats your laundry!

* * *

Definition of a lecture:
  A lecture is something that makes you feel numb at one end and dumb at the other!

Very Sick Jokes

I put spot remover on my dog, and he disappeared!

* * *

There's a new disease in Texas called RAIDS!
Recently Acquired Income Deficiency Syndrome!

* * *

A guy goes to the doctor, and the doctor says, "Sit down, I have some bad news to tell you. I reviewed all your laboratory data, and based on the findings I think you have only six months to live!" The guy says, "Holy shit! That's horrible!" The doctor says, "Yeah, but I have some advice for you. I think you should marry a Jewish girl and move to Cleveland." The guy says, "Is that going to save me?" The doctor says, "No, but it will be the longest six months you ever lived."

What were the last words received from the shuttle Challenger?

"I said, 'A Bud Lite'!"

* * *

Did you hear that Prince Rainier finally got some good news?

The car was covered by insurance!

* * *

A guy goes into an antique shop, looking for a grandfather clock. Sure enough, he finds one that he likes and asks the shop owner how much. The owner says, "Fifteen hundred." The guy tries to barter the price down but can't, so he agrees to pay $1,500 for the clock and then asks the shopkeeper to ship it to his home. The shopkeeper says, "Wait a second. The price doesn't include shipping. We don't ship anything." The guy says, "You're kidding! You mean I have to carry it home all by myself?" The shop owner says, "Well, yeah, but we'll help you get started." So the guy bends over, the shopkeeper puts the grandfather clock on his back, wraps him up with rope and sends him out the door to walk home.

The guy struggles down the road until he comes to an intersection. The light is green, so he starts across the street, but a truck comes barreling down the street, turns the corner and slams right into him. The guy and his clock fly twenty feet in the air, then crash down onto the road, and the clock breaks into a million pieces. The poor guy is very upset, and he screams at the truck driver, "You idiot! Why the hell don't you watch where you're going!" And the truck driver yells back, "Well why don't you wear a wristwatch like everybody else!"

One day Farmer John goes to visit Farmer Bob, and Farmer Bob shows him all around the farm. They come to a pigsty, and Farmer John sees a pig inside with one leg. So he says, "Farmer Bob, you have a beautiful farm here, but how come that pig over there has one leg?" Farmer Bob says, "Well, lemme tell you about that pig. That pig is something else. One day my youngest is out there swimming on the lake and got in trouble and started to go down. That pig went shootin' out of the pigsty, jumped in the lake, swam over to him, dragged back the young'un onto land, resuscitated the child — I never saw nothin' like it. That pig there is something else." And Farmer John says, "Yes, but Farmer Bob, why does that pig have only one leg?" Farmer Bob says, "That pig! That pig is something else! One day the house caught fire, and me and the missus and all the children were upstairs, flames engulfing us, and that pig came flying out of the pigsty, climbed the stairs, grabbed Mother and me, got all the children and dragged us out of the house. Saved all our lives. That pig there, that pig is something else." Farmer John says, "Yeah, but why does that pig have only one leg?" And Farmer Bob says, "That pig! That pig is just terrific. One day little Bobby was walking down the road, and this big tractor trailer was coming. Bobby was a goner for sure and that pig saw it — that pig went flying out of that pigsty, ran down the road, grabbed my little baby, pulled him off the road. Just missed that big old tractor trailer, saved the boy's life. That pig there is something else." "Yeah. But Farmer Bob, why does that pig have only one leg?" Farmer Bob says, "Well, pigs like that, you can't eat 'em all at once."

A guy goes to the doctor, and the doctor says,"Sit down. I have good news and bad news for you, and I'll tell you the bad news first. I reviewed your lab tests, your chest X-ray, your EKG's, and they look real bad. You only have a couple of weeks to live." The guy says, "Holy shit! That's the bad news? What's the good news?" The doctor says, "You know my new receptionist? The girl out there with the red dress and the big tits? I'm fucking her."

* * *

What do you get when you cross a pickle and a deer?

A dildo!

* * *

The doctor says, "I don't advise surgery. I think you should massage your breasts every morning when you get up and repeat,'Little itty-bitty, I must rub my titties,' over and over while you do it." So every morning the girl gets up, and the first thing she does is rub her breasts and say, "Little itty-bitty, I must rub my titties." One morning she wakes up late and in the confusion she forgets to do her exercise — she showers, runs out of the house and just manages to catch her bus. Then she remembers, "Oh, my God! I have to do my exercise. The doctor said if I don't do it every day it won't work." So she starts to rub her breasts on the bus, muttering softly,"Little itty-bitty, I must rub my titties." The guy in the seat behind her overhears this, and he leans forward and says, "What are you doing?" And the girl, embarrassed, says "None of your business!" The guy says, "Wait a minute. Do you go to see Dr. Smith?" And the girl says, "How do you know?" And the guy says, "Hickory dickory dock!"

What did Grace Kelly have that Natalie Wood could have used?
A good stroke!

* * *

How can you tell if you are overweight?
If you step on your dog's tail and he dies!

* * *

Why was time-out called in the leper hockey game?
There was a face-off in the corner!

* * *

How can you tell if a Valentine is from a leper?
The tongue's in the envelope!

* * *

What's blue and comes in Brownies?
Cub Scouts!

* * *

Why is sex like a bridge game?
You don't need a partner if you have a good hand!

* * *

What's the definition of mixed emotions?
When you see your mother-in-law backing off a cliff in your brand-new Mercedes!

* * *

What's brown, soft and sits on a piano bench?
Beethoven's First Movement!

What's big and white and lives on the bottom of the ocean?

Ku Klux Clam!

* * *

What's the definition of gross?

When you open up your refrigerator and your rump roast farts at you!

* * *

Why does Helen Keller have a yellow leg?

Because her dog is blind too!

* * *

How do you tell if you have bad acne?

If a blind man reads your face!

* * *

Did you hear about the new deodorant called Umpire?

It's for foul balls!

* * *

What's brown and sounds like a doorbell?

Dung!

* * *

How do you circumcise a whale?

Send down fore-skin divers!

* * *

Why aren't cowboys circumcised?

So they have someplace to keep their Skoal when they're eating!

How do you make a baby float?
One root beer and two scoops of baby!

* * *

What did the red worm say to the caterpillar?
"What did you have to do to get that fur coat?"

* * *

Why are mopeds and fat ladies similar?
They are both fun to ride, but you don't want your friends to see you on either one!

* * *

What's black and crispy and comes on a stick?
Joan of Arc!

* * *

Why do gorillas have big nostrils?
Because their fingers are so big!

* * *

Why does Helen Keller masturbate with only one hand?
So she can moan with the other!

* * *

What's yellow and sleeps alone?
Yoko Ono!

* * *

What's the difference between a hog and a man?
A hog doesn't have to sit in a bar and buy drinks all night just so he can fuck some pig!

What do you get when you mix holy water with castor oil?

A religious movement!

* * *

What has orange hair, green feet and comes out of a test tube?

Bozo the Clone!

* * *

Why is there so little fraternizing on naval ships?

Because they seldom see each other face to face!

* * *

What do women and streets have in common?

They both have manholes!

* * *

Three nuns have lived chaste, celibate lives, and one day they decide to do something devilish. They part and decide to meet back in a week to tell each other how they've sinned. A week passes, and the nuns get together, and the first nun says, "I put a rubber in the priest's drawer." The second nun says, "I poked holes in it." The third nun faints!

* * *

A woman goes into a butcher shop and asks for a Long Island duck. The butcher thinks to himself, "She'll never know the difference.... I'll give her a Maine duck." So he gives her a Maine duck and she feels up the duck's ass, and says, "This isn't a Long Island duck, this is a Maine duck!" The butcher has only one Long Island duck, and he doesn't want to part with it, so he gives her a Vermont duck.

The woman feels up the duck's ass again and says, "This isn't a Long Island duck, it's a Vermont duck." By this time the butcher is so impressed with the lady's knowledge of duck that he decides to give her the Long Island duck. So he gives the duck to her and she feels up it's ass and pronounces, "This is definitely Long Island duck." Then she says to the butcher, "By the way, where are you from?" And the butcher bends over and says, "You tell me!"

* * *

While two nuns were walking through the park, they both got raped. After they pulled themselves together, one nun asked the other, "Should we tell the Reverend Mother that we were raped twice?" The other nun replied, "What do you mean raped twice? We were only raped once." The first nun said, "Well, we're walking back the same way, aren't we?"

* * *

A man has lived a very bad life on earth, and when he comes before God, he is sent to hell. The devil meets him and says, "You have three choices, but I just wanted to let you know, once you decide, that's it. You have to spend eternity in that manner. Here are three doors, and I want you to choose how you're going to spend eternity." The man opens up the first door, and it's a vast room with thousands of people standing on their heads on a cement floor. The guy thinks to himself, "No, this cement floor looks pretty bad." He then asks the devil if he can see what's behind door number two. The devil opens it, and the guy looks in and it's another vast, room with thousands of people standing on their heads on a wooden floor. The guy thinks to himself that wood is a little softer than cement, but for all of eternity...? No thanks. He finally says, "What's behind door number three?" The devil opens the third door, and all these people are standing knee-deep in shit, drinking coffee. The guy thinks, "Well I could get used to the smell, and they are drinking coffee and having a pretty good time talking." He says, "This is how I want to spend eternity!" The devil says, "Are you sure?" The man says, "Sure!" So the man wades in the shit, and he stands there and has a cup of coffee, and he's talking with some people. Suddenly, after five minutes, the devil opens the door and says, "Coffee break's over! Everybody on your head!"

* * *

Did you hear about how the hot-dog vendor found out if his wife had a boy or a girl?

He said, "So, Doc, with or without?"

* * *

There's a blind guy who has a seeing-eye dog, and he is poking around the supermarket. He takes his dog by the tail and starts swinging it around over his head. The manager comes up to him and says, "Hey, wait a minute buddy, what are you doing?" The man says, "Just taking a look around!"

* * *

There's a boy who is eternally optimistic, and his uncle gets really mad at him because no matter what happens, no matter how bad it is, the boy is always happy and laughing. So, to get back at him, his uncle fills the boy's room with horseshit up to the ceiling. He waits outside until the boy comes home. When the boy opens his door, he shouts, "Wow! This is great!" The uncle runs in and screams, "Great? What do you mean great? It's a pile of horseshit!" The kid says, "With all the shit in here, there's gotta be a horse somewhere!"

* * *

What's the definition of a virgin in Appalachia?
  A girl who can outrun her uncle!

* * *

Why do they call camels "ships of the desert"?
  Because they're filled with Arab semen!

* * *

Two old baseball fanatics developed a pact whereby if one of them died first, he would return to earth and tell the other whether or not baseball existed in heaven. Well, the first man died and did indeed return with good news and bad news for his friend. "Well," he said, "The good news is that they do have baseball in heaven." His friend said, "Well, what's the bad news?" The first man said, "There's a game tomorrow, and you're pitching!"

* * *

How did the dead baby cross the road?
  He was stapled to the chicken!

* * *

How did Helen Keller burn her fingers?
  She was trying to read the waffle iron!

There's this snail who wants to buy a Datsun 280Z. So one day he's going past the showroom and he sees a red Z car in the window, and he goes in and asks the salesman the price. The salesman quotes him a price of $28,000. The snail says, "I'll buy it!" The salesman is a little perplexed, and he asks, "You got the money?" The snail says, "Sure!" and gives the salesman $28,000 in cash. He says, "But one thing. Can you do me one favor? Can you change the 'Z' to an 'S'?" The salesman calls in his mechanic, asks him if he can make the change, the mechanic does so, and the snail happily gets in the car. He drives out of the showroom, puts the car in first gear, and lays a patch of rubber twenty feet down the road. He shifts into second, and lays a patch of rubber fifteen feet down the road. In third gear the snail leaves a patch of rubber ten feet down the road. He shifts into fourth and is gone in a cloud of dust. The mechanic turns to the salesman and says, "Holy Smokes! Did you see that S-Car-Go!"

* * *

Did you hear about the neo-Nazi who was a bigot and a bed wetter?

He went to Ku Klux Klan meetings in a rubber sheet!

* * *

Jacques goes into a bar and says to the bartender, "I'll bet you $100 that I can stand on this barstool, spin around and then pee into a shot glass without one drop spilling anywhere else." So the bartender says, "Sure, let's go for it." Jacques gets on the stool, spins around and then pees all over the place —

all over the bar and the bartender. The bartender can't help laughing at the sight of Jacques. So Jacques loses the bet, hands the bartender his $100, and the bartender asks, "Why did you bet such a stupid thing buddy?" And Jacques replies, "Stupid? It's not stupid. I just bet those two men over there $500 that I could pee all over you and make you laugh!"

* * *

My wife said, "I haven't been myself lately."
I said, "Congratulations on the improvement!"

* * *

Harry, the dairy farmer's son, decided to get off by attaching the milk machine to his dick. It was great. Now he knew why the cows would come home to be milked. But then Harry ran into trouble. The darn contraption was stuck to his dick. It was an automatic milker and Harry knew that he was in trouble. Luckily, his father happened to come into the barn at that time and could not help but notice his son's problem. With the automatic milker stuck to his son's dick, how was he going to milk the cows? The troubled farmer phoned the salesman who sold him the machine. "Listen," he shouted, "it's an emergency. My son got his dick caught up to the milking machine and now he's stuck. What should we do?" "Well, you'd better bring in some strippers to run naked through your barn and tickle his toes and kiss his ears!" "Why?" asked the farmer. "Because that milking machine is automatically set to turn off when it fills a gallon!"

Man to his doctor: "Well, Doc, do you think I'll live?"

Doctor: "Yes....But I wouldn't advise it!"

* * *

Did you hear about the chicken that crossed the basketball court?

He heard the referee was blowing foul!

* * *

Did you hear about the dummy in the outhouse who put one leg in each hole and shit in his pants?

* * *

Do you know what you call twenty-five fat ladies swimming in a pool?

The Bay of Pigs!

* * *

How does an idiot take a shower?

He pees in a fan!

* * *

I met a man in a bar last night who said, "I'm from Buffalo."

"That's funny," I said. "I'm from normal parents!"

* * *

I made a working agreement with my wife.... She works, I agree!

* * *

Did you hear about the man who lost the left half of his body?

He's all right now!

What substantial evidence is there that the sanitation department designed the female anatomy?

They put a waste disposal near a recreational area!

* * *

A mortician is examining a cadaver with the biggest penis he has ever seen. He calls to his assistant upstairs and says, "You've got to come down and see this!" The assistant comes down, the mortician shows him the penis and says, "Did you ever see anything like it?" The assistant replies, "I've got one like that." The surprised mortician says, "That BIG?" And the assistant replies, "No, dead!"

* * *

Did you ever read *Jump Off the Cliff?* by Hugo First?

* * *

Have you read *Suicide* by Eileen Dover?

* * *

Did you read *The Tiger's Revenge* by Claude Balls?

* * *

Have you read the novel *Yellow Stream* by I. P. Daly?

* * *

I'm reading a book called *Castration* by Kutchakockoff!

Did you hear about the great new tranquilizer?
It's called Damnitol!

* * *

You're in the good hands of Allstate until you have an accident.... Then you get the finger!

* * *

A notice reads:
LION TAMER WANTS TAMER LION!

* * *

A man had insomnia so bad that even when he slept he dreamt he didn't!

* * *

A billing clerk went to a psychiatrist.... He kept hearing strange invoices!

* * *

A groundhog came out at Central Park and was immediately rolled by a mole and a few young robins!

* * *

A woman thought she had bought a gown for a ridiculous price when actually she bought it for an absurd figure!

* * *

Two expectant fathers are pacing the floor of a maternity ward.

One says, "Don't I have the worst luck? This is my vacation."

The other says, "You should complain. This is our honeymoon!"